# RAND

# *The Redesign of Governance in Higher Education*

*Roger Benjamin, Stephen Carroll,
Maryann Jacobi, Cathy Krop,
Michael Shires*

*Supported by the
Lilly Endowment Inc.*

**Institute on
Education and Training**

RAND's Institute on Education and Training conducts policy analysis to help improve education and training for all Americans.

The Institute examines *all* forms of education and training that people may get during their lives. These include formal schooling from preschool through college; employer-provided training (civilian and military); postgraduate education; proprietary trade schools; and the informal learning that occurs in families, in communities, and with exposure to the media. Reexamining the field's most basic premises, the Institute goes beyond the narrow concerns of each component to view the education and training enterprise as a whole. It pays special attention to how the parts of the enterprise affect one another and how they are shaped by the larger environment. The Institute

- Examines the performance of the education and training system
- Analyzes problems and issues raised by economic, demographic, and national security trends
- Evaluates the impact of policies on broad, system-wide concerns
- Helps decisionmakers formulate and implement effective solutions.

To ensure that its research affects policy and practice, the Institute conducts outreach and disseminates findings to policymakers, educators, researchers, and the public. It also trains policy analysts in the field of education.

RAND is a private, nonprofit institution, incorporated in 1948, which engages in nonpartisan research and analysis on problems of national security and the public welfare. The Institute builds on RAND's long tradition—interdisciplinary, empirical research held to the highest standards of quality, objectivity, and independence.

# PREFACE

This report argues that a set of fundamental changes underlies the growing number of critical difficulties American higher education faces. The governance system—the written and unwritten policies, procedures, and decisionmaking units that control resource allocation with and among institutions—is inadequate to deal with the changed environment. The study suggests guidelines for higher education leaders now coping with the effects of the changed environment. The study is part of a project on "Redesigning Higher Education" sponsored by the RAND Institute on Education and Training with funds from a grant by the Lilly Endowment Inc.

The study contributes to the restructuring of higher education institutions and postsecondary systems. The report should also be of interest to those parties interested in the broader question of restructuring public institutions.

# CONTENTS

Preface . . . . . . . . . . . . . . . . . . . . . . . . . . . . . . . . . . . . . . . . . iii

Figures and Table . . . . . . . . . . . . . . . . . . . . . . . . . . . . . . . vii

Summary . . . . . . . . . . . . . . . . . . . . . . . . . . . . . . . . . . . . . . ix

Acknowledgments . . . . . . . . . . . . . . . . . . . . . . . . . . . . . . . xiii

Chapter One
    INTRODUCTION . . . . . . . . . . . . . . . . . . . . . . . . . . . . . 1

Chapter Two
    HIGHER EDUCATION IN AMERICA . . . . . . . . . . . . . . . . 5
    The Higher Education Sector . . . . . . . . . . . . . . . . . . . . . . 5
    Fiscal Problems . . . . . . . . . . . . . . . . . . . . . . . . . . . . . . . 7
    Access Concerns . . . . . . . . . . . . . . . . . . . . . . . . . . . . . . 8
    Meeting the Needs of Minority Students . . . . . . . . . . . . . 9
    Quality Concerns . . . . . . . . . . . . . . . . . . . . . . . . . . . . . . 10
    Contributions to Science and Technology . . . . . . . . . . . . 10
    Turnover in Leadership . . . . . . . . . . . . . . . . . . . . . . . . . . 11

Chapter Three
    THE CHANGED ENVIRONMENT . . . . . . . . . . . . . . . . . . . 13
    The Role of the Higher Education Sector . . . . . . . . . . . . . 13
    Changing Student Demographics . . . . . . . . . . . . . . . . . . . 14
    Demands for Research and Service . . . . . . . . . . . . . . . . . . 16
    Technology . . . . . . . . . . . . . . . . . . . . . . . . . . . . . . . . . . . 17
    Finances . . . . . . . . . . . . . . . . . . . . . . . . . . . . . . . . . . . . . 17
    Costs . . . . . . . . . . . . . . . . . . . . . . . . . . . . . . . . . . . . . . . . 19
    The Challenge of the Changed Environment . . . . . . . . . . . 21

Chapter Four
RESOURCE ALLOCATION IN HIGHER EDUCATION . . . .    23
The Current Governance System . . . . . . . . . . . . . . . . . .    23
Limitations of the Current Governance System . . . . . . . .    28
Process Flaws in the Current System . . . . . . . . . . . . . . .    28
Four Examples of the Limitations of the Current
    Governance System . . . . . . . . . . . . . . . . . . . . . . . .    31
    The Inability to Set Priorities Within an Institution . . . .    31
    The Inability to Set Priorities Among Institutions . . . . . .    32
    The Lack of Comparative Tools . . . . . . . . . . . . . . . . . .    33
    The Inability to Implement Priorities . . . . . . . . . . . . .    33
The Fundamental Problem: An Inadequate Governance
    System . . . . . . . . . . . . . . . . . . . . . . . . . . . . . . . . . .    34

Chapter Five
NEW GOVERNANCE SYSTEMS: GUIDELINES FOR
CHANGE . . . . . . . . . . . . . . . . . . . . . . . . . . . . . . . . . . .    35
The Context . . . . . . . . . . . . . . . . . . . . . . . . . . . . . . . .    36
Basic Elements of Reformed Governance . . . . . . . . . . . .    37
Improving the Ability of Higher Education to Set
    Priorities . . . . . . . . . . . . . . . . . . . . . . . . . . . . . . . . .    37
Obtaining Comparative Information . . . . . . . . . . . . . . . .    39
Overcoming Constraints . . . . . . . . . . . . . . . . . . . . . . . .    40
Guidelines for the Change Process . . . . . . . . . . . . . . . . .    41
Corollaries . . . . . . . . . . . . . . . . . . . . . . . . . . . . . . . . .    44
Conclusion . . . . . . . . . . . . . . . . . . . . . . . . . . . . . . . . .    45

Bibliography . . . . . . . . . . . . . . . . . . . . . . . . . . . . . . . . . .    47

# FIGURES

1. Annual Average Growth in Enrollments . . . . . . . . . . .  15
2. Higher Education Resources' Average
   Annual Growth . . . . . . . . . . . . . . . . . . . . . . . . . . . .  18
3. Average Annual Change in Real Faculty Salaries . . . . .  20
4. Organizational Chart:  The College of Letters
   and Science . . . . . . . . . . . . . . . . . . . . . . . . . . . . . . .  26
5. Percentage Change in Constant Dollars per Student,
   1971–1987 . . . . . . . . . . . . . . . . . . . . . . . . . . . . . . . .  31

# TABLE

1. Revenues . . . . . . . . . . . . . . . . . . . . . . . . . . . . . . . .  6

There is increasing concern over the health of higher education in America. As a result of fiscal constraints, colleges and universities are retrenching, cutting back enrollments, reducing course offerings, increasing class size, deferring facility maintenance, reducing library acquisitions, postponing the acquisition of needed research and instructional equipment, freezing and cutting salaries, and cutting faculty and staff. These cuts also threaten access to postsecondary education for students from middle- and low-income families. At the same time, there are widespread concerns that: (1) the quality of undergraduate education has eroded over the past two decades; (2) higher education's response to minorities remains inadequate; (3) the production of scientists and engineers is insufficient to meet national needs; and (4) the quality of American research and development may be deteriorating in comparison with that of competitors.

Our preliminary research strongly suggests that many of these problems are effects of a set of fundamental changes in higher education's environment. Higher education is faced with an increasingly diverse student population, new and changing demands from society, limited or even declining resources, and escalating costs. Changes in any one of these dimensions would present a significant new challenge to higher education. However, the combination of changes now under way adds up to a whole that exceeds the capacity of the current system.

To effectively respond to the changing environment, higher education must be able to reallocate resources from low to high priorities, focus missions, and implement choices. Unfortunately, the track record of higher education institutions and postsecondary systems in accomplishing these tasks is poor. The governance system—the policies, procedures, and decisionmaking units that, taken together, control the allocation of resources within and among postsecondary institutions—is inadequate. The current governance system evolved in response to the problem of managing growth. It is incremental, equipped to add, say, 5 percent to already existing budgets or make across-the-board cuts. To state the situation more explicitly, this governance system is structured to deal with an environment that no longer exists.

An improved governance system is necessary so that higher education leaders can transform their institutions to address the problems effectively.

In fact, the overall effects of the changed environment are forcing redesign of existing governance systems within and across postsecondary education systems throughout the country. The problem is that higher education policymakers at all levels are focusing on cutting costs without sufficient regard to defining missions, reallocating resources, and making choices among the present activities in which higher education institutions are engaged.

This report suggests guidelines for higher education leaders now faced with the necessity of dealing with the changed environment. First, improvements in the governance system can neither be top-down nor bottom-up: they must be interactive. Second, to ensure cooperation by all academic and administrative units in planning and priority setting, all participants must have a role in forming the rules of the process. The planning and priority-setting process must be university-wide: All units must be asked to participate. Third, the planning and priority-setting process should be conducted to provide as much open information and discussion as possible. Initial recommendations of faculty task forces and central administrators should be public and preliminary so as to allow affected units to rebut and reply. Appeal mechanisms must be put in place to allow units that are affected by tentative recommendations to respond.

Among the reasons for these guidelines is our assumption that no one small group of decisionmakers has sufficient knowledge to set priorities and reallocate resources within today's highly complex higher education and postsecondary institutions. The focus should, therefore, be on creating the best possible process through which priorities can be set and resources (re)allocated. Thus, the focus of higher education leaders should be on higher education's governance system: how it functions and how it might be changed to cope more effectively with the challenges of the changed environment.

# ACKNOWLEDGMENTS

We thank John Brademus, Miles Brand, Richard Cyert, Kenneth Gross-Lewis, Kenneth Keller, Theodore Marmor, John Porter, Arnold Shore, and Harold Shapiro for their valuable comments on an earlier draft. Our RAND colleagues Bruce Bimber, David Finegold, David Lyon, Louise Parker, Cathleen Stasz, and Georges Vernez provided criticism, support, and encouragement throughout the study.

# Chapter One

# INTRODUCTION

Near the beginning of the twenty-first century, higher education remains one of America's greatest strengths. For well over a century, our higher education institutions have provided an ever increasing number of students with an education that allowed them to achieve their individual aspirations for a better life. In turn, the United States has become the preeminent economy in the world. Many of the world's scientific advances occur in American university laboratories. While few international students come to study in American primary and secondary schools, millions have attended U.S. colleges and universities. The American higher education sector has set the standards for equity and access for all citizens and for excellence in academic achievement.

There are ominous signs, however, that the higher education sector is no longer able to respond to new challenges as vigorously and effectively as in the past. Indeed, an increasing number of commentaries point to clear signs of deterioration that warrant attention. Observers differ in the problems they emphasize and the solutions they offer. However, many observers' concerns, though important in their own right, are symptoms or effects of a fundamental disjunction between higher education's changing environment and its governance system—the constellation of written and unwritten policies, procedures, and decisionmaking units that control resource allocation within and among higher education institutions at all levels.

The challenge to higher education emanates from dramatic changes simultaneously occurring in its role in society, the demographic composition of students, societal demands for research and service, the costs of instruction and research, and the availability of public support. Any one of these changes by itself would present significant new challenges to the sector. However, the combination of changes now under way adds up to a fundamental transformation.

To effectively respond to these changes, higher education institutions and systems must be able to reallocate limited resources among competing demands. New demands require new responses that, in turn, require new combinations of inputs. However, because resources are limited, changes in the input mix can be accomplished only by redirecting resources.

Unfortunately, higher education does not have a good track record in the reallocation of resources. Examples of gross misallocations of resources are common. While some of these examples can be traced to poor or inattentive management, most stem from a deeper, more fundamental problem: The existing governance system in higher education, designed to manage growth, cannot effectively cope with the problem of reallocating resources. It cannot meet the challenges of the rapidly changing environment. The central issue is how to design improved governance tools that will allow decisionmakers to more effectively reallocate resources from low to high priorities and focus missions within and among higher education institutions.

This places the policy focus squarely on governance. A redesigned governance system is a prerequisite to effectively responding to the various problems threatening the sector. In fact, the long-term question of whether higher education's governance system needs to be restructured is largely moot. Current fiscal pressures, accelerating the long-term changes, are already forcing higher education institutions and systems across the country to restructure. And there are no signs of fiscal relief anytime in the foreseeable future. If anything, the numbers of institutions and systems forced to address the problems of identifying priorities, focusing on central missions, and reallocating resources are likely to grow. The central question is how, not whether, higher education's governance system should be restructured to provide,

- At the national level, an appropriate federal government role

- At the state level, better differentiation of missions among postsecondary institutions

- At the institutional level, improved organizational designs and decision support systems and more focused mission differentiation.

The purpose of this report is to develop and justify a thesis concerning the fundamental problems facing higher education. We believe the thesis is sufficiently novel to warrant exposition now in hopes of stimulating comments and criticism. We also note, however, that we are at the beginning, not the end, of a substantial program of research on the subject that must be carried out to more fully corroborate the thesis. This particularly includes more precise solutions. The available data are not sufficient to conclusively demonstrate the validity of our thesis. And we presently lack the information necessary to identify the most appropriate responses to the rapidly changing environment.[1] However, higher education leaders are now confronted with difficult problems that must be addressed in the near term. This report offers our analysis of the problems that now confront higher education, our diagnosis, and the policy guidelines that follow from the thesis.

Chapter Two places the higher education sector in its larger social context and catalogues the major problems observers believe threaten the sector. Chapter Three presents evidence for the changed environment thesis that suggests that resource allocation is the key. Chapter Four presents illustrations of higher education's ineffectiveness in (re)allocating resources and focuses on the deeper,

---

[1]We are beginning a number of research projects designed to corroborate the changed environment thesis, to model existing resource allocation mechanisms, and to design, and assist in the implementation of, new governance structures.

Our principal unit of analysis is the higher education institution set within the system of postsecondary education institutions of the state to which they belong. The framework encourages constituent parts to think about their particular comparative advantage. Thus, departments are examined in the context of the institution, public or private, and institutions are examined in the context of the postsecondary system to which they belong. Each system is to be analyzed in the context of the overall ecology of higher education in the state. So, for example, we are interested in mission differentiation questions between departments within higher education institutions and between the community college and university systems within the state. By comparison, Massy and his colleagues (see the basic references for this group in Odden, 1992) are developing a profitable research program focused on the department as the principal unit of analysis. The two units of analysis are complementary; one takes the other as largely given. For justification for the focus on the institution as the appropriate unit of analysis in policy research, see March and Olsen, 1989, and Moe, 1984.

underlying source of the problems facing the higher education sector:  the current governance system.  Chapter Five proposes guidelines for higher education leaders that follow from, or are implied by, the argument.

# HIGHER EDUCATION IN AMERICA

## THE HIGHER EDUCATION SECTOR

Higher education in America is a major enterprise. In 1989 just over 13.5 million students were enrolled in the nation's 3,500 public and private colleges and universities.[1] Most of these students, about 11.7 million, were undergraduates; about 1.8 million students were enrolled in professional and graduate programs. Private colleges and universities accounted for about 20 percent of total enrollments.

Higher education institutions employed over 2.3 million people. Just over one-third of the total were faculty. Administrators, research and instructional assistants, and other professional staff numbered about 650,000. Higher education employed almost 900,000 nonprofessional staff.

Table 1 shows the sources of the sector's $140 billion in current fund revenues (1989). The public good aspect of higher education is reflected in the 42 percent share of higher education's current revenues provided directly by federal, state, and local governments. Federal and state governments also indirectly support higher education by providing grants and subsidizing loans to students to help them pay their tuition and fees. State governments are the most important source of direct support to higher education, accounting for

---

[1]The data presented in this section are from the National Center for Education Statistics (NCES), *Digest of Education Statistics,* 1992, various tables.

## Table 1

### Revenues

| Source | Revenues (in billions of dollars) | Revenues (percentage) |
|---|---|---|
| Federal government | 17 | 12 |
| State government | 38 | 27 |
| Local government | 4 | 3 |
| Tuition and fees | 34 | 24 |
| Sales and services | 31 | 22 |
| Private gifts, grants, and contracts | 8 | 6 |
| Other | 8 | 6 |

$38 billion. Over 90 percent of these funds are provided in the form of appropriations to public colleges and universities. Of the $17 billion that the federal government provides directly to higher education, most, about $13 billion, is restricted grants and contracts, primarily for research, and support for federally funded research and development centers. The federal government also provides about $12 billion in student financial aid, about half in the form of grants to students and about half in the form of subsidies for work-study and student loan programs. Local governments contribute about $4 billion, mostly in support of public two-year institutions.

Colleges and universities earned over $31 billion from sales and services. A substantial fraction of these funds were fees levied by university hospitals. Tuition and fee revenues to higher education institutions added up to about $34 billion, just under a quarter of their current fund revenues. Students and their families provided about $27 billion of these funds; the remainder came from the federal government's $6 billion in direct federal student financial aid. Private gifts, including endowment income, grants, and contracts, and other sources of current fund revenue made up the remaining $17 billion in higher education's 1989 current fund budget.

There are growing indications that the health of the American higher education sector is in jeopardy: Fiscal problems now confront public and private institutions across the entire country. The resulting budget reductions threaten to plunge the sector into confusion and chaos. Moreover, there are growing concerns about low- and middle-income students' access to higher education, the extent to which the sector is meeting the needs of minority students, the quality of undergraduate education, the sector's contribution to the competitiveness of the American economy, and leadership turnover.

## FISCAL PROBLEMS

Thirty-six states have cut their higher education budgets over the past two years (Jaschik, 1992). A recent American Council of Education (ACE) survey (El-Khawas, 1992) reports that 57 percent of U.S. colleges and universities reduced their operating budgets during the 1991–1992 academic year, even more than the 45 percent that did so in the 1990–1991 school year. According to this survey, the majority of the nation's colleges and universities—73 percent of public two-year schools, 61 percent of public four-year institutions, and over one-third of U.S. private institutions—had to reduce operating budgets during the past year. As a result of these cutbacks, colleges and universities are retrenching, cutting back enrollments, reducing course offerings, increasing class size, deferring facility maintenance, reducing library acquisitions, postponing the acquisition of needed research and instructional equipment, freezing and cutting salaries, and cutting faculty and staff.[2]

These responses are not self-evidently negative: If the sector were overbuilt, for example, cutbacks might be highly desirable, eliminating excess and waste. Or if overly generous governmental support for higher education had resulted in inappropriately low costs to students and, consequently, enrollments in excess of socially desirable

---

[2]California's recent experience is representative of the impacts that fiscal constraints have on higher education: In 1992, California's community colleges received no state funding for 88,000 students and had to increase fees 20 percent. The California State University system canceled 4,000 classes, sent layoff notices to over 1,300 tenure-track faculty, and increased fees 40 percent. One institution proposed the elimination of nine academic departments and termination of 150 tenured faculty. Another proposed terminating all library acquisitions. A third suggested dropping 639 class sections. A fourth proposed terminating all temporary and part-time faculty. The University of California system responded to budget cuts by increasing fees 24 percent, on the heels of a 20 percent fee increase in the previous year. In addition, attractive voluntary retirement packages have resulted in hundreds of senior faculty early retirements without regard to the size, type, or quality of each faculty member's unit. Virtually every other state's higher education system is experiencing similar problems.

levels, shifting the revenue base away from public support and toward higher tuition and fees might result in a more efficient system. And there may well be other arguments in support of greater fiscal constraints on higher education.

However, these cutbacks and fee increases do not reflect public policy choices regarding either the appropriate size of the nation's higher education sector or the degree to which public support of higher education is overly generous. If anything, a variety of current concerns underscores the importance of an expanding higher education sector for the well-being of the American economy, society, and polity.[3] Further, there is no evidence that higher education's responses to fiscal constraints have been effective. There is no compelling evidence that the cuts higher education systems and institutions have made to date are focused on areas of waste and excess, or that the increased reliance on private support for the sector has resulted in greater efficiency or responsiveness. However appropriate fiscal constraints might be in the abstract, there remains the question of whether the sector has either the incentive to respond in ways that best serve the public interest or the tools needed to implement appropriate responses.

## ACCESS CONCERNS

When government funding falls, higher education institutions are forced to seek financing from other sources. The most obvious solution is to impose student fee increases. Between 1979 and 1989, the cost of attending a public or private college rose by over 109 and 145

---

[3]Higher education is the linchpin necessary, if not sufficient, as infrastructure for economic growth and international competition. Moreover, postsecondary education remains the principal mechanism for social mobility for all ethnic groups and social classes in American society. As such, access to colleges and universities is a major public policy concern. Higher education is an indispensable element in the reform of K–12 education. Higher education's admissions and curricular requirements are important leveraging mechanisms affecting what is taught in high schools. And higher education is both the source of future K–12 teachers, and thus the primary determinant of their capabilities, and the primary mechanism for improving the skills of current teachers.

percent, respectively. In contrast, the Consumer Price Index rose about 64 percent over the same period. Rates of increase in tuition and fees have outpaced health care increases over the past decade (Hauptman, 1991). This trend appears to be accelerating. The ACE (El-Khawas, 1992) reports that 81 percent of public four-year colleges and universities and 55 percent of private colleges and universities raised tuition over the past two years.

One has only to reach for the nearest newspaper to verify that this trend continues unabated. Unless colleges and universities find additional sources of institutional support, or can reduce the relative cost of producing an education, we can extrapolate from a decade of indicators to predict a future of continued fee increases. These increases threaten access for low- and middle-income students.

## MEETING THE NEEDS OF MINORITY STUDENTS

There have been dramatic increases in access of African-American and Hispanic students to postsecondary institutions over the past five decades. Nonetheless, serving the needs of minority students adequately remains an unfulfilled goal. Participation rates of African-American and Hispanic students remain well below those of white and Asian-American students (Koretz, 1990). For example, 16 percent of Hispanic 18–24 year olds and 25 percent of African-Americans were enrolled in college in 1990, compared with 33 percent of whites in this age group enrolled in college. Strong gains in minority enrollment rates seen in the 1960s and 1970s appear to be leveling off, and in some cases even declining.

Rates of achievement, retention, and graduation are lower among African-Americans and Hispanics than whites or Asian-American students (Eaton, 1992; Finn, 1992). Among students who started at a four-year college or university in 1980, fewer than one-half of African-Americans and Hispanics had completed a degree by 1986 (Porter, 1989). Also, participation of minorities in graduate education continues to be low. In fact, the number of African-American doctoral degree recipients actually dropped between 1977 and 1990 (from 1,253 to 1,145) (NCES, 1988–1991).

## QUALITY CONCERNS

Criticism of the quality of education, especially undergraduate education, delivered by our nation's colleges and universities has increased over the past decade. Only about half of the students entering four-year colleges and universities will earn degrees, and the time needed to earn a baccalaureate degree is increasing, especially at public universities. In addition, critics contend that many of those students who do get B.A.s have failed to master skills in writing, quantitative analysis, and critical thinking.[4]

Quality concerns span a wide variety of issues, including: declining student achievement, the apparent decline of liberal education (and concomitant rise in vocationalism), the rise in employment of part-time faculty, the increasingly impersonal undergraduate education, the decline in the numbers of students majoring in science and mathematics, the divisive effects of Eurocentrism on the one hand and "political correctness" on the other, the imbalance between faculty teaching and research activities, and the philosophical underpinnings of the educational system.[5]

## CONTRIBUTIONS TO SCIENCE AND TECHNOLOGY

Scientific and technological knowledge is critical to the ability of the United States to compete in a global economy. The future of science and engineering research and education in the United States hinges on the production of the next generation of scientists and engineers. And much of the research that underlies advances in knowledge is conducted within the sector. There are serious concerns about the

---

[4]Over one-half of a national sample of college upper-class students were unable to perform cognitive tasks at a high school level; three-quarters of faculty surveyed in a recent poll felt that their students did not meet minimum preparation standards; and a growing proportion of students required remedial instruction. In three out of ten campuses, more than one-half of the freshmen require remedial work. See Finn, 1992.

[5]See, for example: NIE, 1984; Bennett, 1984; Smelser, 1986; Bloom, 1987; Boyer, 1987; Porter, 1989; Carnegie Foundation, 1990; Pew Higher Education Research Program, 1990; Duster, 1991; and Richardson, 1991. The business community has also expressed considerable concern about the preparedness of college graduates, especially with regard to their analytic and communication skills (cf., Finn, 1992).

ability of the sector to fulfill these missions as effectively as needed to improve, or even maintain, the nation's competitiveness.

The number of doctorates awarded by American universities in mathematics, engineering, and the physical sciences declined throughout the 1970s. Although the downward trend was reversed in 1980 and the number of Ph.D.s awarded in these critical fields has slowly grown through the 1980s, the production of new Ph.D.s in 1989 had barely regained that of 20 years earlier. The story is much the same with respect to the production of new Ph.D.s in the life sciences, an area many expect will become the most important technological frontier. Here, too, the numbers of doctorates awarded by American universities peaked in the early 1970s and has not increased since then (NCES, *Digest of Education Statistics*, various years).[6]

The eventual impact of declines in the numbers of Americans earning Ph.D.s in the sciences and engineering is uncertain. But the steady decline in the numbers of American citizens completing Ph.D.s in these critical fields raises the possibility of serious adverse future trends in the quality of both science education and research in the United States and, consequently, on the production of scientific and technological knowledge.

## TURNOVER IN LEADERSHIP

The difficulties that now confront higher education are reflected in the turnover rates for presidents of the nation's campuses (Leatherman, 1992). Leadership instability rises when institutional problems become less tractable. We found that more than one in four of the public institutions listed as Research University I in the Carnegie Classifications that hired a chancellor in the 1980s needed to look for a replacement within three years. Similarly, 22 percent of those who assumed the presidency of a major research university

---

[6]The problem may be even more serious than implied by the gross trends in Ph.D. production. An increasing proportion of the new doctorates awarded each year in these fields has been earned by foreign nationals. For example, more than half of the doctorates awarded in engineering in 1989 were to non-U.S. citizens (Ottinger, 1991). U.S. students are not completing Ph.D.s in mathematics, engineering, and the sciences in sufficient numbers to meet national needs (Bowen and Rudenstine, 1991).

sometime in the 1980s left their posts within three years. (If those appointed as "acting" or "interim" presidents were included, this percentage would increase to 32 percent.)

In contrast, during the 1970s, only 13 percent of the institutions in our sample needed to replace a newly hired chancellor within three years. And only 15 percent of the individuals who assumed the presidency of a major research university sometime in the 1970s left their posts within three years.

Given the time needed to create change in higher education, and given the expense and disruption associated with hiring new leaders, this increased turnover represents a substantial loss to the sector and a warning signal for the future.

# Chapter Three

# THE CHANGED ENVIRONMENT

Each of the problems facing higher education, from fiscal cuts to concerns about the quality of undergraduate education, is important in its own right and warrants attention. These concerns take on a much greater importance, however, when considered as a whole. They are symptoms of a fundamental transformation in higher education's environment. Recent economic, demographic, political, and social changes in American society have come together to dramatically alter both the purposes the sector is asked to serve and the resources available to it. Higher education is now faced with a new set of social roles and responsibilities, an increasingly diverse student population, new and changing demands from both students and society, limited or declining resources, and escalating costs. Together, these changes compose a fundamentally new set of challenges to the higher education sector.

## THE ROLE OF THE HIGHER EDUCATION SECTOR

For two centuries following the founding of Harvard in 1636, the American higher education system comprised small, private colleges that focused on meeting the needs of an agrarian society. For the most part, they provided a "classical" education to a small number of citizens, primarily the sons of the wealthy. The society looked to the higher education system to provide professionals—ministers, doctors, and lawyers—and the political and social leadership to guide a new nation.

In 1826, Thomas Jefferson initiated a redefinition of the role of American higher education. Jefferson saw mass public education as a way to provide the educated citizenry needed for economic development and democracy. His bold argument placed the future of the country squarely in the hands of a system that provided practical "technical" education at low cost to a sizable fraction of the population. The institutional inspiration, the land grant university, was founded on the principles of access and excellence—access for all qualified applicants combined with the opportunity to achieve to one's fullest intellectual capacity. The state-based structure Jefferson's heirs adopted, rather than a national-based governance model, made sense in a time when communication and coordination across a diverse and vast continent were difficult, and the structure was appropriate for an economy relatively sheltered from global competition.

Now, however, society's demands on higher education are changing yet again. An individual's opportunity to pursue his or her goals continues to be an important public policy objective. However, the implication of this goal for the higher education system is very different from what it has been. Today the system is expected to prepare the next generation of Americans to live in an interdependent world in an information-centered economy. In addition, as the American economy goes global and moves more centrally into the information age, higher education is increasingly perceived as America's principal point of comparative advantage against international competitors. Human capital is clearly becoming the central engine for economic growth, and human capital is the main product of higher education.

## CHANGING STUDENT DEMOGRAPHICS

One of the most dramatic changes in the higher education environment has been the sharp decline in the rate of enrollment growth since the mid-1970s. Fueled by a combination of rapid growth in the traditional college-aged population and dramatic increases in participation by other groups, enrollments in colleges and universities grew rapidly from the turn of the century until World War II and soared through the 1960s and into the early 1970s. The rate of growth in enrollments then flattened dramatically, averaging between 1 and 2 percent through the late 1970s and the 1980s. (See Figure 1.)

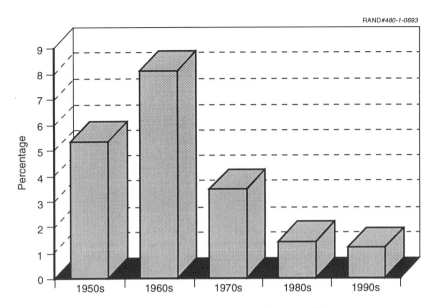

Figure 1—Annual Average Growth in Enrollments

Most of the increases in enrollments since the mid-1970s resulted from increasing participation by nontraditional groups in the sector. While detailed data on students' characteristics are not available prior to 1965, the changes since then are dramatic. The proportion of students who are female, older, minority, or part-time has grown considerably both absolutely and relative to their respective male, younger, white, or full-time counterparts. The number of female students has increased from 38 percent of the student population in 1962 to 54 percent in 1990. The number of students over the age of 35 has risen from 4 percent in 1965 to 19 percent in 1990 and is projected to rise to 24 percent by the turn of the century. Minority enrollments accounted for 19 percent of the student body in 1990, a level up from 6 percent in 1965 and expected to rise to 26 percent by the year 2000. Finally, part-time enrollments have risen from less than 30 percent in 1965 to more than 43 percent in 1990.

This growth in traditionally underrepresented populations is simultaneously one of the most impressive achievements and most difficult challenges of the higher education sector. Diversity has invigorated many campuses, and higher education is increasingly available to those who would once have been denied access. However, increased diversity presents new demands on higher education because of changing student needs, values, and aspirations. Some of these changes stem from students' increasing need to balance school, work, and family obligations. Some stem from increasing numbers of underprepared students entering the higher education sector. Others reflect fundamental challenges to the nature and substance of intellectual inquiry. But, regardless of the source of these changes, traditional ways of doing business are proving increasingly inadequate.

## DEMANDS FOR RESEARCH AND SERVICE

The changes in demands for research and services provided by higher education are striking as well. Societal demands for basic research continue unabated. At the same time, there have been important new demands placed on the postsecondary education sector. Increasingly, universities are expected to address the societal issues of the day—everything from the causes of urban riots in Los Angeles to the need for a vaccine for AIDS. While universities are expected to continue research on field theory in physics, they are now also expected to make breakthroughs in applied fields, such as superconductivity, that give promise of generating new practical applications. Moreover, through university/industry partnerships and even start-up companies, higher education institutions are increasingly asked to directly stimulate local or state economic growth.

The pattern is similar with respect to demands for services. Familiar services, such as agricultural extension and continuing education, remain important ingredients in the service mix of many institutions. There also continues to be a steady increase in the number and types of miscellaneous services higher education institutions are expected to provide their communities. For example, universities are hosts for radio stations, elder hostels, airports, a variety of cultural centers, and real estate services. The list is very long. Finally, universities are increasingly expected to provide pro bono consulting and technical service to all levels of government.

## TECHNOLOGY

Higher education's environment is profoundly affected by changes in technology. Advances in data storage, analytic speed and capabilities, and communications are having major impacts on instruction, research, and, increasingly, administration. The new technologies have already significantly transformed scholarship, and this process is expected to continue. Technology and innovations in research methodologies, library resources, dissemination of information, and worldwide communication and collaboration among researchers create adaptive challenges for higher education, ranging from the costs of providing faculty with hardware, software, and user support services to the transformation of basic mission and functioning of the research library. Similarly, administration is undergoing fundamental modifications due to new technologies.

Although new technologies may greatly increase access to higher education and improve the quality of instruction, their adoption poses obvious technical and financial challenges. In addition to assuming hardware costs, institutions or systems must support staff and faculty in developing applications, modify pedagogy, adapt or renovate classroom space to accommodate computer technology, provide user support services, and maintain equipment and software.

## FINANCES

Higher education was awash in "new public money" through the three decades following World War II. While the numbers of students to be served grew rapidly, the revenues governments made available for higher education grew even faster, even after adjusting for inflation. (See Figure 2.) With substantial increases in real public resources, colleges and universities could readily accommodate to changing growth demands and without recourse to increased tuition and fees. The issue of where to cut expenditures rarely arose. Rather, the dominant problem was which of many new activities would be initiated this year and which would have to be deferred to a future date.

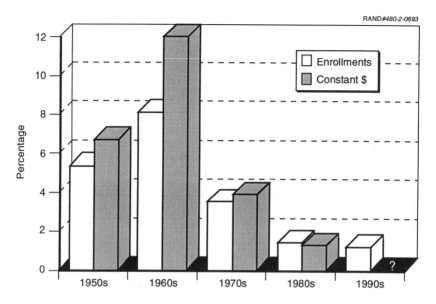

**Figure 2—Higher Education Resources' Average Annual Growth**

This picture changed dramatically in the late 1970s. The rate of growth in the real resources governments provided to higher education fell sharply, averaging 1.8 percent from 1975 to 1990. Because the rate of growth in enrollments also fell sharply, real public resources per student continued to increase through the late 1970s and the 1980s, but at much lower rates than those experienced in the prior three decades. Estimates of higher education's likely future revenues from governmental sources are not now available, but there is no reason to expect a turnaround anytime soon.[1] Thus, it appears that higher education is going to experience a lengthy period of slow growth, if not outright declines, in real public revenues per student.

---

[1]We believe the recent cutbacks in public support to higher education are long term in nature and not a function of the recent recession. The trend toward slower growth in public support to higher education was under way well before the current recession. Furthermore, this slowdown came not only at the federal level, but also at the state and local levels, reflecting the increased competition for public resources overall. As the ACE study indicated, there is little or no evidence, at least at the crucial state and local levels, that the level of support for higher education is likely to increase as the country emerges from recession.

The mid-1970s slowdown in revenue growth introduced an entirely new era. The combination of slowly growing enrollments and minute increases in real revenues per student means that there is very little annual growth in the real resources available to the sector. There is little "new money." Simultaneously, new and more demands are placed upon the sector. In this environment, these new activities can be supported only by cutting support for preexisting activities. Thus, the problem facing higher education decisionmakers is whether, not when, a new demand should be met and, if so, which current activities should be cut back or terminated to accommodate the new activity.

## COSTS

Concurrent with this slowdown in the level of resources committed to higher education is significant evidence that the costs of providing higher education are far outstripping inflation. For example, faculty salaries, a major component of higher education's costs, did not keep pace with inflation in the 1965–1979 period.[2] They have grown at an average annual rate that exceeded the rate of inflation since then. (See Figure 3.)

The costs of other goods and services particularly important to higher education have also increased more rapidly than inflation over the last couple of decades. For example, National Science Foundation (Office of Technology Assessment, 1991) estimates imply that the cost (in 1988 constant dollars) of equipping a full-time investigator in the physical or natural sciences has risen from $85,000 in 1958 to $225,000 in 1989. Notwithstanding improvements in the equipment available for the faculty, which are reflected in the quality of the research produced, the costs of the research equipment needed by the average investigator in these fields have increased about two and one-half times faster than inflation over this time period.

---

[2]Rank-specific data on faculty salaries are not readily available prior to 1965. Growth rates cited here are calculated from data in the NCES, *Digest of Education Statistics*, various years and tables.

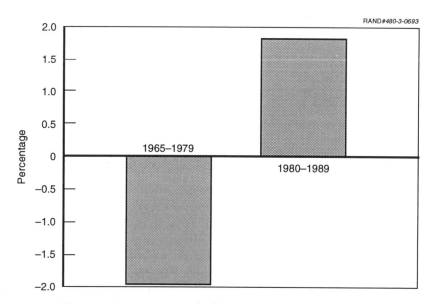

**Figure 3—Average Annual Change in Real Faculty Salaries**

Similarly, a private research university built a brand new, state-of-the-art medical school in the early 1960s at a total cost of approximately $75 million (in 1988 constant dollars). That expenditure included the physical plant and all equipment and facilities. In 1989, that university budgeted $170 million (in 1988 constant dollars) for the modifications and upgrades needed to maintain its medical school at the state of the art.[3]

Other higher education costs grew more rapidly than inflation in the 1970s and 1980s as well. The costs of journals and books have grown at or above inflation rates over the past 15 years. And many well-established higher education institutions began to face serious physical plant repair and maintenance issues in the 1980s, the result

---

[3]An important task is to collect, organize, and interpret the disparate data on research and physical plant costs. One hypothesis, uncorroborated, is that costs of research equipment began to escalate to virtually exponential levels in the 1980s in the wake of the telecommunications revolution, and increases in size and capitalization of scientific equipment. We see this analysis as a high priority of our future research.

of decades of neglect and accounting practices that did not provide for physical capital depreciation.

## THE CHALLENGE OF THE CHANGED ENVIRONMENT

Society continues to expect higher education to respond to traditional demands for instruction, research, and service but also expects the postsecondary sector to meet a wide variety of new demands as well. The sector's resources, however, are not growing as fast as are the demands it is expected to meet. If anything, the purchasing power of the resources available to higher education per student is declining.

To be sure, higher education organizations are not passive recipients of environmental forces. They may strive to modify or influence public perceptions and expectations of higher education;[4] they can also attempt to increase the resources available to the sector.[5] Although such efforts might ease pressures on the system for a time, they do not address the fundamental problem of allocating limited resources among competing demands. The demands on the sector reflect social needs. Reducing demands on higher education implies that important social needs go unmet. Tuition and fee increases similarly substitute one problem, access, for another, revenue shortfalls. Higher education may be able to increase its revenues by offering new services. But the resources that must be devoted to the provision of new services will consume much of whatever new revenues are thereby generated, leaving the problem of how to best allocate preexisting revenues among preexisting demands.

Higher education institutions and systems can also attempt to make better use of their resources through increased efficiency. For exam-

---

[4]Higher education leaders have attempted to shape demands on the system through activities ranging from lobbying legislatures and negotiation with state-wide higher education coordination commissions to direct appeals to the public. They may also choose to disregard specific expectations or demands, generally in the hope that the demand will pass and business as usual can resume.

[5]Colleges and universities have responded to fiscal constraints with tuition increases, fundraising campaigns, the development of new markets (e.g., adult students) or new "products" (e.g., new extension services or degree programs), partnerships with business and industry, or the imposition of new fees for services that were formerly covered by general fees and tuition (e.g., health services and career workshops).

ple, institutions have increased class sizes or asked faculty to teach extra courses. Yet asking faculty and staff to "do more with less" has obvious limits, as well as negative effects on the quality of instruction and research. Higher education systems and institutions may generate cost savings through freezes on hiring, equipment purchases, and travel; on work furloughs; or on incentives for early retirement. These and other methods may cut costs in the short run, but the results may leave critical functions unfulfilled, impose heavy burdens on some staff and faculty, and limit the ability of the institution to pursue quality or excellence. Further, unless those costs were for entirely unnecessary activities, quality must eventually suffer.

In any event, regardless of institutions' and systems' success in reducing expectations, attracting increased revenues, and improving efficiency, the sector is now faced with new and changing demands from both students and society, limited or even declining resources, and escalating costs. To effectively respond to changing demands, higher education institutions and systems must be able to (re)allocate their limited resources among competing demands. The primary management challenge facing higher education leaders is to allocate the available resources in ways that best meet the demands placed on the sector.

# Chapter Four

# RESOURCE ALLOCATION IN HIGHER EDUCATION

We use the term "governance system" to refer to the constellation of policies, procedures (written and unwritten), and decisionmaking units that control resource allocation within and among higher education institutions at all levels. The current governance system evolved in an environment of relatively stable growth. Incremental,[1] decentralized decisionmaking became the dominant approach to allocating resources within and among postsecondary institutions. This approach served well in an era of stable growth. But it is poorly suited for setting priorities and reallocating resources. Here, then, is our argument, followed by illustrative evidence.

## THE CURRENT GOVERNANCE SYSTEM

The current governance system evolved in an environment of rapid, sustained growth. Budgets grew as fast as did enrollments. Any changes in students' demands could be accommodated by increases in overall budgets; there was little need to think of reallocating resources from existing programs to new ones. Because state-level administrators were focused on expanding overall capacity to keep

---

[1]The classic explication of incremental decisionmaking remains Lindblom, 1959. There are a number of themes in recent work in organization theory to be researched further to corroborate the arguments and assertions made here. There is a good deal of current interest in restructuring governance in the private sector. The question is the extent to which this work provides guidance for our topic. For representative citations see Istvan (1992) and Ostroff and Smith (1992). There is a longer tradition of studies of decentralized decisionmaking relevant to the public sector to examine; see Pateman (1970).

pace with enrollment growth, resource allocation among institutions was largely ad hoc. Little attention was given to differentiation of mission between institutions. Finally, the federal government took no responsibility for the overall health of the system; the federal government remains focused on higher education primarily as a means for the pursuit of specific national objectives such as scientific advancement and national security.

Most higher education institutions and systems evolved decentralized and "stovepiped" governance structures in which organizational entities or components, such as departments, which may themselves employ participatory decisionmaking principles, report to higher-level organizations with little communication between entities at the same level. The specifics differ across higher education systems and institutions. Context, history, tradition, size, complexity, and mission are all important considerations. However, irrespective of the many differences among institutions and systems, the common principles, routines, and practices of the governance structures found in most higher education institutions and systems constrain reallocation of resources and, in so doing, limit higher education's ability to adjust to a changed environment.

The governance system that emerged to deal with the problem of growth was and remains *incremental*, equipped to add, for example, 5 percent onto already existing budgets or to add new functions without subtracting existing ones.

The governance system is also *decentralized* in that individual units and departments have a great deal of autonomy over how they allocate their resources. In the typical institution or system, the various academic and administrative units operate independently and in isolation from one another. Within a single university, for example, the Dean of the College of Arts and Sciences may allocate resources among the several dozen social science, humanities, life science, and physical science departments; the Dean of Engineering may do the same for a variety of engineering programs; and the Vice President for Operations may do the same for such departments as facilities maintenance, parking, and campus security. Yet these processes occur largely in isolation from one another. Further, each academic department has considerable independence in decisionmaking about how to use its allocation. Departments generally make major decisions regarding goals, curricula, and new hires, internally, with subsequent review and refinement by the faculty senate and/or academic administration. For example, the academic departments within most institutions not only recommend the specialty of the faculty to be hired but the minimum number required and their preferred rank.

Yet, the governance system is *hierarchical* in the sense that departmental chairs report to deans who, in turn, report to vice presidents. The collegiate or administrative units report up or down but tend not to be connected across to collateral collegiate or administrative units. At the system and state level the salient characteristics of the governance system are similar. The central administrators of the community college system report to a state postsecondary authority but typically have little or no relationship with the state college or university systems within their states. And the university system leaders similarly have little or no knowledge of the state college or community college systems.

Even those leaders at the very top of the governance hierarchy, however, must build coalitions with administrative and faculty leaders to implement change successfully. Higher education governance is largely consensual, and few presidents or chancellors can impose their will without the support of the faculty senate and other key decisionmaking groups. Consensual decisionmaking generally acts as a conservative force, slowing the rate of change, avoiding extremes, and protecting the pursuit of multiple goals and objectives.

Another salient characteristic of higher education governance is its *complexity*, particularly within large research universities. Figure 4 displays the organization chart of a representative College of Letters and Science in a major research university. Although this chart is complex itself, it does not reflect the larger institutional, state, or federal context. For example, the unit shown is one of over a dozen colleges within this institution. And, outside the institution, accrediting agencies, the state legislature, and a variety of special interest and advocacy groups exert pressure and sometimes require the college to respond to demands ranging from the content and rigor of the curriculum to the number of books in the library. It is difficult to imagine how to manage this structure effectively.

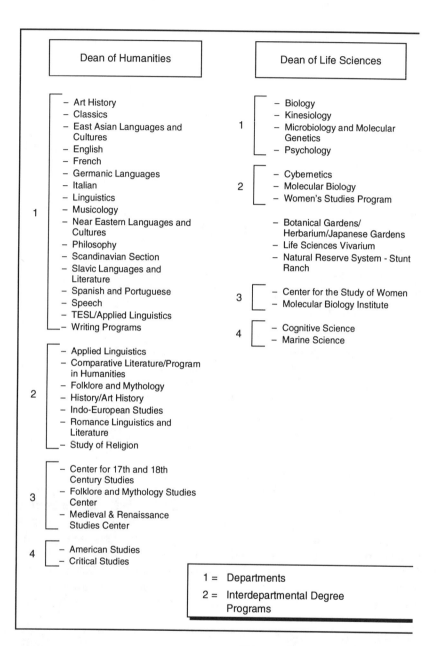

**Figure 4—Organizational Chart:**

RAND#480-4-0693

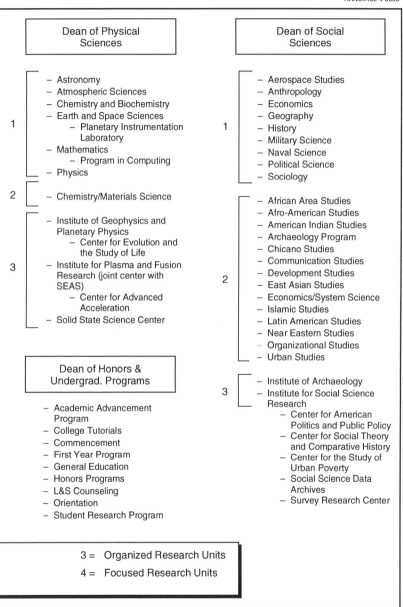

## The College of Letters and Science

## LIMITATIONS OF THE CURRENT GOVERNANCE SYSTEM

The current governance system presents severe challenges to the administrators of any college or university confronted with changing demands and limited resources. For example, the current financial climate forces administrators to consider such trade-offs as whether the institution should hire an assistant professor of classics, provide resources for research equipment for a physics institute, or provide funding for more student counselors. The incremental, decentralized, and consensual nature of decisionmaking has enabled the institution to pursue multiple goals and directions for many years, so there is likely to be considerable disagreement about decisionmaking criteria. The complexity and weak horizontal linkages further increase the difficulty of conducting comparative analyses to assess the relative merits of the competing proposals. And the influence of various stakeholder and constituent groups may reduce the real options open to administrators and force them to pursue particular paths.

## PROCESS FLAWS IN THE CURRENT SYSTEM

The current decentralized, hierarchical governance system virtually makes inevitable the inability of institutions and systems to set priorities, focus missions, and implement choices among academic programs. We noted above that the current governance system gives a substantial amount of autonomy to departments in resource allocation. Negotiation about allocation decisions is two-way, with messages going up to the dean or down to the department. This is the system that served institutions well in the earlier period of growth. It is serviceable for operating in a steady-state environment. And in the early stages of fiscal cutbacks, academic units can absorb mandated across-the-board cuts. If fiscal cuts continue long enough however, the perverse effects of across-the-board cuts become clear and salient enough to persuade most participants in the governance system that another method of resource allocation is needed.

As higher education systems and institutions seek alternative approaches to resource allocation, however, they face additional obstacles stemming from the governance system. The characteristics of the governance system described here lead to "top-down" and "bottom-up" decisionmaking processes—i.e., communication flows along narrow vertical columns, with few feedback loops or horizontal linkages.

The department-centered, bottom-up governance structure is ill equipped to meet the challenges of resource reallocation in a rapidly changing environment. Economists, for example, may be able to persuasively argue the necessity of econometrics, given the presence of an economics department. They may be able to point to minimum critical mass required for an economics department to cover the agreed upon core undergraduate and graduate curriculum of economics—agreed upon by economists. Economists are also considered the best judge of the research quality of economists' publications and, therefore, are best suited to deciding whom to hire and recommend for tenure and promotion. But economists have little experience, standing, or competence concerning the same decisions regarding the classics department. In other words, economists can make the case for their unit but do not have the decisionmaking evaluation criteria or information useful in evaluating the case for the classics department or, more important, for comparing the cases of the two units.

When faced with the need to go beyond the across-the-board cuts strategy necessary for the current governance system, a department-based, bottom-up solution is not feasible. Indeed, this conclusion is what typically leads to the error most frequently committed when higher education institutions are faced with the necessity of choice, the top-down strategy.

When faced with the necessity of choice, the only decisionmakers with formal authority and relevant information are deans and/or central administrators. Indeed, under immediate threat of fiscal cutbacks, central administrators do propose sweeping cuts of entire departments, professional schools, collegiate units, or even branch campuses. Such attempts virtually always fail to be carried out. And they fail for the same reasons that department-based solutions are doomed: absence of comparative information and decisionmaking evaluation criteria. Because central administrators are accustomed to operating in vertical relationships with academic units under their authority, they also lack the means to compare the costs and benefits of hiring an economist versus a classicist. Thus, when central administrators do attempt to establish priorities and implement selective cuts in academic programs, they are vulnerable to criticism from below to a number of arguments.

First, academic units argue that cost criteria are not enough for establishing priorities, that each unit is unique; i.e., only economists can judge the qualifications of economists. Thus, each academic unit targeted for cuts invariably can and does make a strong case for the preservation or enhancement of its program, based on absolute criteria, e.g., the department of speech communication shows that it is important to the goals of research, teaching, and service and, moreover, shows that this particular department of speech communication needs only steady-state funding to maintain its present quality, or it needs additional funding to increase its quality. The academic units selected by central administrators for fiscal cuts or elimination also argue that they were not given an opportunity to present their case based on their data and their criteria. This usually is a strong argument because appropriate statistical information concerning cost of the academic program, faculty/student ratios, and output measures are seldom collected routinely by central administrators. Moreover, because central administrators have targeted particular academic units for cuts, those units then can argue that potential alternative cuts of other units have not been adequately explored and that they have been unfairly singled out.

The top-down solution is, therefore, usually rejected by the faculty, many of whom have tenure, who successfully argue that the top-down strategy and recommendations are illegitimate, that they violate the collegial decentralized nature of the governance structure in place. Indeed, there are significant numbers of higher education institutions that have been damaged by top-down efforts that were eventually aborted but that nonetheless have left individual academic units weakened because of negative publicity, the sense of collegiality between departments and central administrators destroyed, and the reputation of the institution as a whole weakened. Attempts at setting priorities, a mission, and implementation of choices that fail to be implemented can create more problems for the institution than it faced before it began the process of setting priorities.

## FOUR EXAMPLES OF THE LIMITATIONS OF THE CURRENT GOVERNANCE SYSTEM

The following examples, derived from case studies of two states' higher education systems, demonstrate the problems that result from a governance system that impedes reallocation of resources in the face of a rapidly changing environment.[2]

### The Inability to Set Priorities Within an Institution

Figure 5 presents the percentage changes in per student expenditures (constant dollars per student) from 1971 to 1987 for five col-

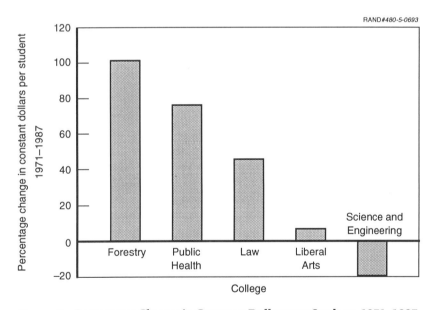

**Figure 5—Percentage Change in Constant Dollars per Student, 1971–1987**

---

[2]The sources for the examples can be obtained from the authors. The data are from nonproprietary sources. However, the data are used here for illustrative purposes only, and the authors do not wish to particularly call attention to any specific institution.

leges within a major public research university. Although the 77 percent increase in the public health field is congruent with the growing national importance of the field, other results are less easily explained. For example, the 104 percent increase in the Forestry field appears discrepant with the declining importance of the field both nationally and state-wide during this time period. Conversely, despite the growing importance of the sciences, expenditures in this field declined over 20 percent.

Resource allocation in this institution has been incremental and decentralized, driven by a combination of tradition and politics. The shifts in resources evidenced in Figure 5 do not reflect deliberate choices to emphasize some areas (e.g., Forestry) at the expense of others (e.g., Science and Engineering). Rather, student preferences changed over time, but the resource allocations to colleges were "locked in" and were not shifted to follow the changes in enrollment patterns. Decreasing numbers of students enrolled in the College of Forestry while the number of students enrolled in the College of Science and Engineering increased. But the university lacked the capacity to shift resources in accordance with shifting student demands. Had the resource allocation process been guided by institutional goals and priorities, the results would most likely have been very different. Further, had university decisionmakers had access to comparative trends, such as those provided in Figure 5, they might have recognized the need to better align expenditures with priorities. In the absence of this information, however, they failed to recognize the cumulative consequences of their incremental decisions.

## The Inability to Set Priorities Among Institutions

The anticipation of deep cuts in a particular state's higher education budget forced each of the campuses in the state's university system to consider how it might achieve cuts of over 10 percent. The planning process and its results are noteworthy for each university's general neglect of institutional, system-wide, or state goals. Each campus planned independently of the others, and there was little to no effort to develop a coordinated response. Further, the campuses developed a wide variety of plans to achieve their budget cuts, the vast majority of which focused on cost criteria and political factors to the exclusion of other possible factors. For example, one administration planned to eliminate several departments where the most expensive faculty were located, although these departments were basic to the ability of the institution to meet its core undergraduate teaching mission. Campus resistance to this plan ensured that it would not be implemented. The result was a drop in morale, worsening of relations between faculty and administration, loss of some of the most talented and productive faculty, and intervention by the system-wide administration. The campus still lacks a plan for achieving future budget cuts. Another campus planned to eliminate all part-time faculty despite the fact that these instructors teach the greatest number of sections and courses at the most cost-effective rates. Another planned to eliminate all library acquisitions—a fundamental component of the research and undergraduate teaching mission. In each case, the retrenchment plans reflected political agendas and expediency—not a strategic analysis of the institution's or the system's mission.

## The Lack of Comparative Tools

A particular public flagship university spent $4,300 per student in its liberal arts college in 1988. The same year, one of that state's community colleges spent over $25,000 per student in one of its programs—mobile home repair. We had to conduct a number of fairly complex programming operations on several different databases to obtain these two numbers. Although the comparison itself is quite simple, these two numbers had never appeared on the same page prior to our analysis. State policymakers were both surprised and dismayed by this chart. Because they lack access to the tools and methods for obtaining such comparative information, however, they were unable to determine if funding allocations were congruent with their goals. This incident demonstrates the importance of comparative information.

## The Inability to Implement Priorities

In the mid-1960s, with support from the United States Office of Education and The Ford Foundation, a midwestern research university established a South Asian Studies department. The university hired and then tenured eight faculty members through normal university hiring, tenure, and promotion practices. In the mid-1970s, interest in South Asia waned in the wake of the end of the Vietnam War. The Office of Education and Ford Foundation terminated support for the department. As a result, the university was left with a department with eight faculty members averaging two full-time equivalent students each in 1990.

This example illustrates the constraints and lack of flexibility in resource allocations. Once established, institutional leaders found it close to impossible, and certainly not worth the resistance they would encounter, to modify the structure, mission, or programs of the department.

## THE FUNDAMENTAL PROBLEM: AN INADEQUATE GOVERNANCE SYSTEM

These examples raise questions about the ability of the higher education sector to allocate resources effectively. However, these examples also suggest that difficulties in resource allocation are the result of a deeper, more fundamental problem. In our view, the current governance system is itself the basic problem. As our examples demonstrate, the governance system lacks the ability to set priorities, fails to provide tools for conducting comparative analyses to consider the relative merits of alternative decisions, and is subject to a wide variety of constraints in decisionmaking due to the influence of various interest groups both within and outside the system.

# Chapter Five

# NEW GOVERNANCE SYSTEMS: GUIDELINES
# FOR CHANGE

We suggest that higher education's current governance system is inadequate for strategic reallocation of resources. The changed environment is making redesign of higher education institutions and systems not just necessary but inevitable. The central issue is how to design improved governance tools that will allow decisionmakers to reallocate resources from low to high priorities and to focus missions more clearly within and among higher education institutions.[1]

Should empirical analysis confirm our hypotheses,[2] what are the implications of this approach for policy and practice in higher education? This section describes some of the possible directions for action based on our conceptual framework.[3]

---

[1]We do not argue that changing the governance system will itself suffice to solve the serious set of problems that the higher education sector faces. We do argue that a governance system that permits or compels reallocation is a prerequisite to the solution.

[2]Elsewhere, we have proposed a research program that needs to be carried out to (1) corroborate the changed environment thesis, (2) map patterns of research allocation within higher education institutions and postsecondary systems, (3) derive and evaluate the decisionmaking criteria that are used in making these resource allocations, and (4) develop improved governance models.

[3]The guidelines are directed primarily at changes in the decisionmaking process within institutions. The guidelines do not, for example, tackle the larger issue of recalibrating the basic missions of higher education institutions and postsecondary education systems. The effects of the changed environment thesis may well point to changes of greater magnitude in mission between and among institutions. A perceptive critic of an earlier draft of this report observed that it may no longer be appropriate for so many students to approach the four-year period of the baccalaureate as life

## THE CONTEXT

The current decentralized, incremental governance structure exists in a supportive decisionmaking culture typically shared by faculty if not administrators and staff. Effective innovations must be sensitive to the context—the local environment and culture. The history of education reform repeatedly demonstrates the futility of imposing externally developed "solutions" on an institution or system. It is important to recognize that the only groups appropriate to develop and implement improved governance structures are the constituencies within the existing governance structures of higher education institutions and postsecondary systems.

*Because* there is little or no experience in reallocation, there is likely to be considerable reluctance on the part of all parties, but especially faculty, to allow the decentralized governance system and the culture that supports it to be transformed. The evidence we have about university planning and priority-setting efforts is mixed. Without clear evidence to the contrary, a member of the sociology department is unlikely to view fiscal problems of physical plant administrators as directly linked to the future of the sociology department. Without a sense of how a new governance structure would improve on the present one, faculty are unlikely to abandon the old structure even with all its present flaws.

Most academic planning and priority-setting efforts are "rational" constructs developed by policy analysts. These constructs almost invariably ignore or oversimplify the existing formal and informal political forces that impose determinative constraints on the current governance structures. Under conditions of financial stress, for example, participants—faculty, staff, students, and interest groups—will question even the most basic and apparently neutral information and analyses.

---

enrichment rather than preparation for work. He questioned whether the fact that the baccalaureate is four years (supposedly) in such disparate fields as electrical engineering and Spanish made sense. In our view, even if the critic is correct, a version of the institution-biased guidelines presented below will be necessary to use in, for example, state government-level debates to achieve sufficient agreement that stronger system-level controls on institutions are needed.

The changed environment may provide an opportunity for fundamental restructuring of present governance systems. When retrenchment makes reallocation inevitable, this gives all participants in the current governance system strong incentives to search for a better way to, at a minimum, carry out retrenchments in a less damaging fashion. In other words, we assume that the college or university is a political process as in all other bureaucratic institutions. This means that decisionmakers within the institution or system of institutions have strong incentives to compromise with other co-participants in their bureaucratic unit, to engage in logrolling tactics when faced with conflict, or to make trade-offs with other members of the unit. However, at critical threshold points, the world of policy analysis and the political reality of nonprofit decisionmaking systems can come together, if only for a brief period, to set new assumptions, structures, and procedures by which resource allocation decisions will be made.

## BASIC ELEMENTS OF REFORMED GOVERNANCE

We suggest that reform of the governance system should be directed toward increasing the capacity of the system to strategically deploy resources. To achieve this goal, the system must address the three structural flaws of the current governance system: the inability to set priorities, the lack of comparative information, and a high level of external constraints.[4]

## IMPROVING THE ABILITY OF HIGHER EDUCATION TO SET PRIORITIES

Because past eras of incrementalism enabled higher education to pursue multiple goals simultaneously, it did not need to develop ways to clarify priorities. In the face of retrenchment, however, institutions face new pressure to cut the areas of lowest priority while maintaining the areas of highest priority. Given the absence of any

---

[4]The governance system evolved over the past century, during which time the American higher education system has gained worldwide preeminence. Thus, interventions and modifications to governance must be approached with extreme caution, lest the benefits of the current governance system be lost along with its limitations.

consensus among decisionmakers about what these high- and low-priority areas are, some criteria are needed to establish priorities.

To go beyond the current governance structure requires evaluation criteria that permit comparison, for example, of classics versus economics. However, the development of such comparative evaluation criteria also requires wide discussion in order to generate an agreed upon set of definitions and contexts to which they should apply. The criteria need to reflect the input of diverse units and individuals because they are ultimately a reflection of organizational values.

Although it may seem impossible to develop a set of criteria general enough to evaluate disparate academic units, comparative evaluations must be undertaken. Hence, criteria, however imperfect, must be employed. We propose the following:[5]

1.  *Quality.* This applies to the quality of the faculty (in teaching, research, and service), the students, library collections, and *services provided.* Both locally designed and standardized quality measures can be used. Indicators of quality include faculty publications, patents, and citations; national ratings and rankings; attrition or graduation rates; and results of standardized assessments.

2.  *Centrality.* Each program should be evaluated in terms of its contribution to the mission of the institution, or system. For example, participants could determine the degree to which the program is an essential component of a liberal arts, preprofessional, or professional education that is regarded as central to the institution's or system's mission. The typical institutional mission statement that emphasizes teaching, research, and service may be too broad to provide meaningful guidance in this task. Thus, consideration of other written documents (e.g., strategic plans or accreditation self-studies) as well as discussion among policymakers and practitioners are required.

_____

[5]One of the authors of this report has participated in three exercises in university strategic planning, each of which developed versions of these criteria listed in the same order of importance. Thus, for example, perception that an academic program is of high quality appears to override low scores on the other criteria. So far, an informal survey of strategic planning efforts in Big Ten and a number of other research universities confirms this point.

3. *Demand and Work Load.* Both short-term and long-term demands (increasing, stable, or declining) for each program must be considered in priority setting. Demand indicators might include trends in the number of applications, acceptances, and admissions, as well as trends in students' choice of majors, services performed in support of other programs, instruction of students in or conduct of research for the solution of pressing societal problems, and the prospective market for graduates. Most institutions calculate and track faculty work load (based very generally on the number of courses offered or students enrolled in courses).

4. *Cost-Effectiveness.* Because aspirations are always limited by the resources available, programs must be continually examined to see if more economical or more efficient ways are possible to accomplish the same ends. Yet cost alone must not govern the decision; the effectiveness of the program must also be weighed. When taken together, cost and effectiveness provide one important measure of whether funds are being put to the best use.

5. *Comparative Advantage.* What is the rationale for the program at the institution or system? What are the unique characteristics of each program that make it essential to the community, region, nation, or other programs within the institution or system?

## OBTAINING COMPARATIVE INFORMATION

Following the establishment of agreed upon criteria for establishing priorities, the next step is to assess various departments, divisions, or institutions against the criteria. This process requires standardized, comparative information about each unit. Ideally, multiple measures will be used for each set of criteria, in order to broaden the range of information and increase the validity of overall ratings. The usefulness of comparative information for decisionmaking also requires that the information be publicly available and perceived as accurate and meaningful.

Both quantitative and qualitative data may contribute to the development of this information base. For example, departmental rankings provide quantitative (ordinal) measures of quality, and the ratio of student to faculty FTEs (full-time equivalents) provides a quantitative (interval) measure of work load. On the other hand, centrality or comparative advantage is perhaps best assessed through interviews with preeminent faculty (both within and external to the unit under review), essays prepared by department chairs, or academic program reviews.

The development of criteria for decisionmaking, coupled with information about the extent to which diverse units meet these criteria, greatly enlarges organizational capacity for resource reallocation. When faced with the necessity to make difficult choices, decisionmakers have some analytic tools at their disposal. This is not to say that the political components of decisionmaking can ever be completely overcome. For example, the possibility always exists that the criteria and associated information will be used to legitimize *a priori* decisions. Nonetheless, these tools reduce the likelihood of organizational paralysis and enable disparate units to argue the merits of various decisions based on shared values and information.

## OVERCOMING CONSTRAINTS

Almost every organization needs to contend with constraints and interest group influences. In the absence of clearly articulated priorities and comparative information, however, higher education is especially vulnerable to such influences.

There is no doubt, for example, that tenure acts as a conservative force against, or a drag on, reform efforts in higher education. Once granted, tenure offers professors freedom from almost all attempts to remove them excepting only a variety of personal misconduct charges. Tenure, thus, has become a central ingredient in the current incremental governance system. The inability of administrators to lay off individual professors in the face of fiscal stress is often cited as a rationale for across-the-board cuts. If financial exigency is declared, tenure can be voided and departments and professional schools can be targeted for elimination. However, declaration of financial exigency is seen as a declaration of bankruptcy. There are very few examples of such actions. In our view, the paralysis that declaration of financial exigency induces in decisionmakers outweighs its benefits. It is possible to eliminate departments or target them for reduction in size or restructuring without eliminating tenure. It is also possible to offer faculty only in targeted units the option of moving to another department, early retirement, or voluntary separation. The effectiveness of such strategies, however, requires that the institution (or system) establish and apply criteria for identifying priorities; in the absence of this decisionmaking criteria, fairly applied, efforts to overcome the constraints associated with tenure will be perceived as illegitimate and probably will be defeated.

The standards and evaluative criteria of the accrediting associations also constrain administrative action and may deter restructuring or reallocation efforts. Again, however, the absence of clearly articulated priorities, criteria for decisionmaking about allocation, and information about how disparate units fulfill these criteria leaves central administration officials largely unable to justify actions directed toward reallocation or restructuring. If central administrators possess comparative evaluation criteria and supporting comparative information systems when meeting with accrediting associations, the discussion might be more equal.

Interest groups also exert powerful influences over higher education policies, ranging from admissions policies to partnerships with business. We know from the logic of collective action literature (Olson, 1965, 1983) that single-purpose groups are more effective in organizing and obtaining their goals than larger, multiple-purpose groups. In universities, the only possible safeguard against private interests is more effective institutional arrangements that support university-wide goals as opposed to any particular set of interests. The development and application of comparative decisionmaking evaluation criteria offer a beginning in the reestablishment of university-wide goals.

## GUIDELINES FOR THE CHANGE PROCESS

The current governance structure is unable to support decisionmakers in setting priorities and differentiating missions; nor does it compel or even encourage implementation of any priorities or choices made. Because of this, or perhaps as a function of it, the current governance system does not have in place comparative, university-wide decisionmaking evaluation criteria. When faced with the necessity to reduce budgets in academic units, the preferred strategy by most higher education institutions is typically one of mandating across-the-board fiscal cuts. This strategy is seen as fair because everyone shares the "pain" equally. However, if the fiscal cuts continue long enough and are deep enough, the negative effects of this strategy become clear. For example, to deal with a fiscal crisis, institutions often freeze all faculty vacancies, meaning that all faculty vacancies due to resignations or retirements revert to the control of college or central administration. The problem with this strategy is that it affects large and small departments equally. It falls equally on departments that teach the most or the fewest students. It falls equally on departments that produce the most and least research. And so on. If fiscal stringencies persist, therefore, responsible faculty and administrators begin to weigh alternative strategies, which translates into the need for a governance system that sets priorities, focuses missions, and compels or facilitates implementation of choices made.

On the assumption that the changed environment requires reforms to existing governance systems, we present a set of inferences that either follow logically from our critique or are reasoned inferences from the critique. Here, then, are guidelines for higher education leaders to follow.

First, an improved governance system can neither be top-down or bottom-up. Neither department-based solutions or central administration solutions imposed from above are likely to succeed. A new governance system must be iterative. Central administrators possess a broad perspective on systemic activities and functions. They must have the authority as well as the responsibility to set priorities and reallocate resources from low to high or new priorities between and among the units under their purview. They must provide the leadership to make the reform efforts work. But they will not be empowered to exercise this authority if the academic departments lack the opportunity to contribute to decisionmaking. Only departments really know what their low and high or new priorities are. Consequently, academic departments must be integrally involved in the new governance system in a way that ensures that they have as much of a stake in the governance system as the central administrators. This iterative process is critical to developing the capacity to establish priorities and criteria for decisionmaking.

Second, even if department leaders accept the need for their institution to move beyond across-the-board cuts, they will be reluctant to cooperate unless they have guarantees and incentives as well as the threat of sanctions. This involves establishing a planning and priority setting process viewed as legitimate by all participants. The planning process will vary by institution or postsecondary system but will be composed of the following rules of the game.

The planning and priority setting process must be university-wide, and everyone deemed eligible should be asked to participate on the same basis. This rule ensures that all academic and nonacademic units are subjected to the same comparative scrutiny from the standpoint of the university. Representatives of the units to be evaluated should be asked to help set the guidelines for the planning and priority setting documents each unit submits to central administrators, i.e., deans or vice presidents. The statistical information to be collected and used should be agreed upon by participants as well. Participants should also have a role in deciding the length of the planning and priority setting process—what date it should begin, when preliminary documents must be submitted, when preliminary recommendations from the dean's or vice president's office must be made, etc. Such a governance process envisages central administrators setting priorities and implementing them. However, academic units must be able to propose their plans and priorities and present supporting documentation. Because of the complexity of most higher education institutions and particularly the fact that multiple goals and missions are pursued, multiple review mechanisms are important to build into the planning effort. While central administrators must have final authority to make decisions, deans and vice presidents can appoint blue ribbon faculty committees from faculty assemblies to review and evaluate the planning documents that come forward. While central administrators may deviate from the recommendations of the faculty committees, these committees provide a check on central administrators. And to the extent that the final decisions of central administrators follow the recommendations of the faculty committees, the legitimacy of the decisions is strengthened in the eyes of the faculty.

Third, the question of whether to conduct planning and priority setting processes behind closed doors or to provide as much open information and discussion as possible is always debated at the start of such efforts. Openness brings with it negative publicity for any unit identified as a low priority. There are several arguments, however, for opting for openness. For example, individual faculty, departments, and colleges have legal and political avenues of redress available to them if they can argue that they have not been given due process. Indeed, initial recommendations of faculty task forces and central administrators should be public and preliminary so as to allow affected units to rebut and reply. Thus, appeal mechanisms must be put in place to allow units that are affected by tentative recommendations to respond. After all, the idea behind the new governance system is to set priorities, focus missions, and implement choices, not just to create winners and losers. Achieving consensus on sharp, unevenly distributed cuts may sound impossible. But if the process is well designed, and if participants help design it and participate under rules developed through wide consultation among all levels of decisionmaking, the institution may well accept the results.

In other words, we reject the idea that any one small group of decisionmakers alone can set priorities and reallocate resources in line with a vision that they have created for the large and highly complex higher education institution's organization described in Chapter Four. Thus, the focus should be on creating the best possible process by which priorities can be set. Finally, institutions can improve even while shrinking budgets and cutting back academic programs. If, for example, the missions of a higher education institution are more sharply focused, it may be easier to raise outside funds for an attractively defined set of missions. If at all possible, as well, academic units should be encouraged to put forward ambitious plans that would require increased budgets—as well as listing their low priorities.

## COROLLARIES

Under the assumption that choices will have to be made and the across-the-board strategy has outlived its usefulness, a surprising number of possibly counterintuitive recommendations arise:

1.  The planning and priority-setting process should begin with broad institution-wide reductions, restructuring goals, or new

missions but not specific targets in mind. Every unit should have an equal opportunity to "make its case" in the planning and priority-setting process.

2.  There should not be any closed "star" chambers of administrators or faculty task forces charged with carrying out the priority-setting task.

3.  There should be clear goals—based on what the institution is asked to do, for example, by its board of trustees, the state legislature, or the governor—laid out at the start in terms of the percentage of fiscal cuts to be achieved, missions to be clarified, or new ones to be started.

4.  There should be clear timetables agreed to by participants and adhered to strictly.

5.  The central administrators and the governing board of trustees must agree to accept the set of recommendations and, after initial recommendations have been refined and changed through the several steps of the planning process, allow no exceptions. Because the new governance system produces an institution-wide set of recommendations, changes for one department or college will have an impact on other recommendations.

## CONCLUSION

If the planning and priority-setting process has been well designed, if participants help in designing it and participate under the rules developed through wide consultation among all levels of decisionmaking in the higher education institution, the results are much more likely to be accepted by members of the institution. The members of the academic programs most negatively affected by the final recommendations may not agree, but the central administrators and senior faculty leaders can point to the fairness of the planning and priority-setting process. Central administrators can then generate or retain support for the final recommendations from the faculty senates, assemblies, councils of deans, and, of course, their own boards of trustees.

We have illustrated the guidelines with examples from higher education institutions. The same guidelines apply, in our view, to postsecondary systems and states faced with the same necessity to set priorities, focus missions, and implement choices.

Overall, we have argued that there is a growing list of significant problems that appear to threaten the higher education sector. More important, from our point of view, is a wholesale set of shifts in the environment of higher education, changes that place a premium on the ability of the higher education sector to (re)allocate its resources effectively. Unfortunately, our preliminary research suggests that the higher education sector does not allocate resources effectively. A deeper, more fundamental problem is that the governance system itself is inadequate to deal with this changed environment; the current governance structure does not give higher education leaders the tools to deal with this changed environment. This puts the research focus squarely on governance. We do not argue that a redesigned governance structure will of itself solve the various problems threatening the sector. However, we do argue that a redesigned governance structure is a necessary condition, i.e., a prerequisite, to dealing with the problems more effectively.

We believe, then, that the focus of research should be on higher education's governance system, how it functions, and how it might be changed to cope more effectively with the challenges of this new environment.

# BIBLIOGRAPHY

Bennett, John B., *To Reclaim a Legacy: A Report on the Humanities in Higher Education*, Macmillan, New York, 1984.

Bloom, Allan, *The Closing of the American Mind*, Simon & Schuster, New York, 1987.

Bowen, William G., and Neil Rudenstine, *In Pursuit of the Ph.D.*, Princeton University Press, Princeton, New Jersey, 1991.

Boyer, Ernest L., *College: The Undergraduate Experience in America*, Harper and Row, New York, 1987.

Carnegie Foundation for the Advancement of Teaching, *Campus Life: In Search of Community*, The Carnegie Foundation, Princeton, New Jersey, 1990.

Duster, T., and the Institute for Social Change, *The Diversity Project: Final Report*, University of California, Berkeley, 1991.

Eaton, Judith, "The Evolution of Access Policy: 1965–1991," in The Aspen Institute (ed.), *American Higher Education: Purposes, Problems and Public Perceptions*, Queenstown, Maryland, 1992.

El-Khawas, Elaine, *Higher Education Survey Report No. 82*, American Council of Education, Washington, D.C., July 1992.

Finn, Chester, Jr., "Why Are People Beating Up on Higher Education," in The Aspen Institute (ed.), *American Higher Education: Purposes, Problems and Public Perceptions*, Queenstown, Maryland, 1992.

Hauptman, A. M., "Trends in the Federal and State Financial Commitment to Higher Education," in D. Finifter, R. G. Baldwin, and J. R. Thelin (eds.), *The Uneasy Public Policy Triangle in Higher Education,* American Council on Education, Macmillan Publishing Company, New York, 1991.

Istvan, Richard L., "A New Productivity Paradigm for Competitive Advantage," *Strategic Management Journal,* Vol. 13, 1992, pp. 525–537.

Jaschik, Scott, "1% Decline in State Support for Colleges Thought to Be First 2-Year Drop Ever," *The Chronicle of Higher Education,* October 21, 1992.

Koretz, D. M., *Trends in the Postsecondary Enrollment of Minorities,* RAND, R-3948-FF, August 1990.

Leatherman, C., "Spate of Resignations Prompts Concern About Health of the College Presidency," *Chronicle of Higher Education,* Vol. XXXVIII, June 17, 1992.

Lindblom, Charles E., "The Science of "Muddling Through," *Public Administration Review,* Vol. 19, 1959, pp. 79–88.

March, James G., and Johan P. Olsen, *Rediscovering Institutions: The Organizational Basis of Politics,* The Free Press, New York, 1989.

Moe, Terry M., "The New Economics of Organization," *American Journal of Political Science,* Vol. 28, 1984, pp. 739–777.

Nadler, David A., *Feedback and Organization Development: Using Data-Based Methods,* Addison-Wesley, Reading, Massachusetts, 1977.

National Center for Education Statistics (NCES), *Digest of Education Statistics,* U.S. Department of Education, U.S. Government Printing Office, Washington, D.C., annual.

National Center for Education Statistics (NCES), *The Condition of Education: Postsecondary Education,* Office of Educational Research and Improvement, U.S. Department of Education, U.S. Government Printing Office, Washington, D.C., 1988–1991.

National Science Foundation, *Federal Support to Universities, Colleges, and Nonprofit Institutions: Fiscal Year 1989*, NSF 91-316, Washington, D.C., 1991.

NIE Study Group on the Conditions of Excellence in American Higher Education, *Involvement in Learning: Realizing the Potential of American Higher Education*, National Institute of Education, Washington, D.C., 1984.

Odden, Allan, "Symposium: Micro-Approaches to Educational Productivity," *Educational Evaluation and Policy Analysis*, Vol. 14, No. 4, 1992, pp. 303–305.

Office of Technology Assessment, *Federally Funded Research: Decision for a Decade*, OTA-SET-490, U.S. Government Printing Office, Washington, D.C., May 1991.

Olson, Mancur, *The Logic of Collective Action*, Harvard University Press, Cambridge, Massachusetts, 1965.

Olson, Mancur, *The Rise and Fall of Nations*, Yale University Press, New Haven, Connecticut, 1983.

Ostroff, Frank, and Donald Smith, "Redesigning the Corporation: The Horizontal Organization," *The McKinsey Quarterly*, Vol. 1, 1992, pp. 148–167.

Ottinger, Cecilia A., *The Higher Education Enterprise*, Research Briefs, Vol. 2, No. 8, American Council on Education, Washington, D.C., 1991.

Pateman, Carol, *Participation and Democratic Theory*, Cambridge University Press, Cambridge, England, 1970.

Pew Higher Education Research Program, "Back to Business," *Policy Perspectives*, Vol. 3, No. 1, September 1990, pp. 1–2.

Porter, Oscar F., *Undergraduate Completion and Persistence at Four Year Colleges and Universities*, National Institute of Independent Colleges, Washington, D.C., 1989.

Richardson, Richard C., and Elizabeth F. Skinner, *Achieving Quality and Diversity: Universities in a Multicultural Society*, American

Council on Education, Macmillan Publishing Company, New York, 1991.

Smelser, Neil J., *Lower Division Education in the University of California:   A Report from the Task Force on Lower Division Education*, University of California, Berkeley, 1986.